THE MEANING OF FINDING COINS DISCOVERY JOURNAL

Bring to Light the Heavenly Messages in the Coins You Find

Companion to:
The Meaning of Finding Coins: Messages and Spiritual Insights

Kimberly Ahri

Printed in the United States of America

ISBN-13: 978-1987488319
ISBN-10: 1987488318

DEDICATION

This journal is for all those who delight in the sight of a coin
on the ground, to the coin picker-uppers of the world, the wonder-seekers,
and those who wish to learn more about the divine communication
being offered through coins.

May both the big and small miracles in our wondrous world
find you and fill your heart.

Table of Contents

Welcome to Wonderland / 1

How to Get the Most Out of This Journal / 3

Examples of Communication / 5

Coin Guide:
The Potential Meanings of Your Coins / 6

Quotes & Journal Pages Begin / 8

Continuation Journal Pages / 74

About the Author / 87

About *The Meaning of Finding Coins:*
Messages and Spiritual Insights / 88

Welcome to Wonderland

Welcome to a fun and exciting spiritual journey into the Land of Wonder—a place where divine connection reveals itself all around you.

I created this journal for you after writing *The Meaning of Finding Coins: Messages and Spiritual Insights,* with the hope and intention of making it easy to track, and thereby discern the messages being offered to you when you find a coin.

The key to understanding this heavenly conversation is your attention. When you keep a record of each coin you find and the details surrounding its discovery, it becomes much easier to note the patterns.

In my own life, it was the patterns that helped me realize there's something bigger at work here—something beautiful, nurturing, and guiding. As you fill the pages of this journal, you won't be able to help but be immersed in this awareness.

Whether you have a loved one on the other side connecting with you through coins, or have angel advocates who God has entrusted to help guide you, a coin placed in your path can begin to feel like a welcome hug.

Since I began my own journey of picking up the coins I find, I've experienced guidance, as well as constant comforting reassurance during some of life's most challenging conditions.

The same comfort and reassurance awaits you! I've had the pleasure of watching others awaken to this divine communication and smiled to myself as it cast its glow across their lives. For some, it's been a true life-changer.

The reasons that folks find coins can vary greatly. Some of us fall into very distinct patterns. Some of us receive many different types of messages. This is why a journal is an excellent starting point to uncovering messages that are personal to you.

To help you shed light upon what types of messages you may be receiving I've included many quotes from *The Meaning of Finding Coins: Messages and Spiritual Insights* and condensed the chapters into categories that I've listed within a Coin Guide.

As you read through the material, please trust yourself to recognize what message is right for you. Allow your built-in divine filter (gut instinct) to illuminate the answers for you. If, when you read the Coin Guide, one of the options touches your heart and is similar to your own experience, go with that. If you read a quote that feels right for the circumstance in which you found a coin, trust that feeling. When it comes to deciphering messages, there's no better guide than your feelings.

While this journal has enough information within it to stand alone, it was created as a companion journal. If you'd like more information to help you build confidence in your ability to clearly recognize the meanings and signs around you, check out the original book. It contains angelic messages alongside uplifting true-life stories. Both of which may provide additional clarity.

My spiritual experiences have taught me to honor free will. Therefore, I'm not making the claim that little 'ol me is the end-all and be-all of coin interpretation. Instead, I'm offering possibilities for you to consider, gleaned from many years of paying attention, noticing patterns and listening to the heavenly tutors that guide me. My intention is to get you started with a method of decoding your own messages while having fun doing it.

For those with coin finding experience who are already confident and "in their knowing" about who their coins are from, or what they mean, this journal still has something for you. It's sure to become a treasure once filled with your experiences. Imagine having all the details to enjoy for years to come. You just can't go wrong recording these special moments!

Shall we begin?

How to Get the
Most Out of This Journal

1. Enter the date the coin was found, coin number, information about where it was found, what or who you were thinking about, the year of the coin, and then circle whether the coin was heads or tails up.

2. Write what type of coin you found in the coin section or tape it there. (This journal was created with alternating top and bottom coin areas for those who wish to tape the coin within.)

   These details are the clues that begin to reveal patterns.

   For example, you may begin to notice that when you think about your dad, who is now in Heaven, you often find dimes. Or, after you find a heads up coin of any kind, life seems to follow the occurrence with a happiness windfall. Perhaps when you find nickels, because they seem to be the least commonly found coin, you notice that a sense of wonder always comes over you and you feel ultra-tuned into the splendor of our beautiful world. Or maybe when you've been stressing about money, a pattern of finding pennies all stamped with the same year emerges—a year that was good to you financially. In that case, I'd call that a pattern of financial reassurance. Allow yourself to bask in the memory of abundant times. Let that sensation be the call that goes out to the Universe: I'd like more of the same, please.

3. In the "My Story" section, write down whatever you can remember about the whole circumstance. (There are full-size continuation pages in the back of the journal if you need extra room.) Be sure to record how you came upon your coin and how you felt when you saw it or picked it up. Our feelings are a gold mine of information. They lead to understanding what our personal messages are.

For example, if you were feeling lonely today and now suddenly, after finding a quarter, you shifted into a more hopeful perspective, I'd call that quarter a loving pick-me-up sent by God, your angels, or your loved ones in Heaven. That's a pretty awesome memory to write down and keep close to heart.

4. My suggestion for the last area, after reviewing the Coin Guide, is to choose a category and check one of the boxes: Affirmation, Comfort & Reassurance, Enjoy the Wonder, Financial Reassurance, Hello from Heaven, or Time for Life Review.

If none of the options provided feel like a fit for your specific coin find and your gut instinct comes up with something unique to you, great! Trust that and change the options to suit you. This is about you, my friend. It's your journal. Please personalize it and enjoy!

Examples of Communication

For fun, here are some examples of what I call "An Invitation to a Divine Conversation." Do coins have to fall into these examples in order to count? Nope. I've learned that every coin you find matters. Pick them all up!

❖ You find a coin where you're positive there was none before.

❖ You find coins in odd places—multiple times.

❖ You have trouble explaining to yourself how the coin arrived. The circumstances are that unusual.

❖ A coin arrived "out of thin air."

❖ You find coins every day for a condensed period of time.

❖ You find a coin after thinking about a loved one. It feels as if the coin is in reply to your thoughts.

❖ You think about how long it's been since you found a coin and then find one right away.

❖ You find the same denomination over and over. Just dimes. Just quarters. Just pennies. Just nickels.

❖ You asked a dying loved one to give you a sign that they're still with you. Once they pass over, you begin finding coins in all sorts of random places.

❖ You recently lost a loved one and as soon as they passed, you couldn't help but notice coins everywhere.

❖ You often find change on the ground when you are concerned about your finances.

❖ You have a hectic lifestyle, or are overwhelmed, yet it's entered your busy awareness that you're seeing coins everywhere.

Coin Guide:
The Potential Meanings of Your Coins

Coins sent our way to serve as affirmations may have these characteristics:

- Tend to show up unexpectedly, in divine timing, rather than in response to specific requests for answers.
- Often appear in response to our thoughts. Ask yourself what you were thinking about the moment you found the coin. An affirmation feels like a whisper from the ethers: *You're headed the right way.*
- Bring a feeling of warmth, joy and positivity, like you are being told YES!
- Can be a bit of an art to learn to recognize. Easier if you're a "feeler" rather than a "thinker."

Coins sent our way to offer comfort and reassurance may have these characteristics:

- Show up when we're feeling alone in the world.
- Are meant to provide us with a feeling/sense of support from our Creator, loved ones, angels and spiritual guides.
- Reveal themselves in unique ways when we are looking for a sense of connection.
- May feel like a direct response to our thoughts that we are in need of support or are feeling without direction.
- Can feel like an actual conversation with participation from the other side that feels amusing or playful.

Coins sent our way to reconnect us to the *Wonder of the Life* may have these characteristics:

- The dazzling nature of how, or where the coin was found stirs feelings of delight, fascination, amazement, or joy.
- Show up to bring our awareness to the little miracles around us every day. (A coin where a coin couldn't possibly be is indeed a little miracle.)
- Offer inspiration and hope to *ALL IN NEED,* especially those with chronic illness, the cynical, bored, or disillusioned with life.
- Encourage us to seek more joy and fun in life by giving us a wondrous jump start.
- Invite us to be present in the moment and remember what's magical about life.

Coins sent our way to offer financial reassurance often have these characteristics :

Financial Reassurance

- Show up when we've been fretting about finances or are overly focused on money.
- Serve as a divine response: Our prayers have been heard and noted.
- Encourage us let go of worry, which makes space for the solution to present itself. When we remain open it's easier to notice answers that may come from unexpected sources.
- Cause us to remember that we are not going through this period alone. We have a heavenly support posse with us.
- Remind us to put our faith back into the Creator.

Coins sent from our loved ones on the other side often have these characteristics:

Hello from Heaven

- Begin showing up in noticeable ways after a loved one passes.
- Tend to show up in the same denomination over and over. Most commonly: dimes and pennies. May also be stamped with dates significant to the family.
- Bring a sense of our loved one with them. We can almost feel their energy around when we pick up the coin.
- Show up soon after we have been thinking of our loved one.
- Show up in a way that reminds us of our loved one, perhaps at a place they like, during an activity they love, or leading up to (or during) a special occasion.

Coins sent to inspire us to pause and consider whether we need to make life changes, or to prepare us for life changes, often have these characteristics:

Time for Life Review

- Show up every single day, everywhere you go. The frequency of coin finding is so extraordinary it may feel comical or fill you with awe. Lasts for a noticeable duration like two, four, or six weeks, often stopping abruptly.
- Encourage us to evaluate life circumstances to see if there are areas in which our soul is calling for improvement or seeking a return to harmony.
- May serve as a loving wake-up call for us to elevate our level of self-care. Invites you to ask yourself: Where do I need to begin treating myself with honor?
- Indicate that a heavenly team is in place ready to help if you want to better your life.

"It wasn't until I started picking up every random coin that crossed my path that I began to see a pattern."

Affirmation	Comfort & Reassurance	Enjoy the Wonder	Financial Reassurance	Hello from Heaven	Time for Life Review

My Story

_____

_____

_____

_____

_____

_____

_____

Date found: _____ Coin #_____

Where: _____

What or who I was thinking about :

_____

_____

Year of coin:

Tails up

Heads up

The Coin

"If you find coins after
a loved one has passed
on, consider this message:
While you may not
see me in the physical,
my spirit is alive and
with you."

Date found: _____ Coin #_____

Where: _____

What or who I was thinking about :

_____

_____

Year of coin:

The Coin

Tails up

Heads up

My Story

_____

_____

_____

_____

_____

_____

_____

Affirmation	Comfort & Reassurance	Enjoy the Wonder	Financial Reassurance	Hello from Heaven	Time for Life Review

"If you find coins during times of financial insecurity, consider this message: Your prayers have been heard. You are free to release your worry."

Affirmation	Comfort & Reassurance	Enjoy the Wonder	Financial Reassurance	Hello from Heaven	Time for Life Review

My Story

_____

_____

_____

_____

_____

_____

_____

Date found: _____ Coin #_____

Where: _____

What or who I was thinking about :

_____

_____

Year of coin:

Tails up

Heads up

The Coin

"The comfort offered through found coins can be extremely impactful. A random coin can provide nourishment for the spirit just when it's needed the most."

Date found: _____ Coin # _____

Where: _____

What or who I was thinking about :

_____

_____

Year of coin:

The Coin

Tails up

Heads up

My Story

_____

_____

_____

_____

_____

_____

_____

Affirmation	Comfort & Reassurance	Enjoy the Wonder	Financial Reassurance	Hello from Heaven	Time for Life Review

"The coin that serves as
an affirmation carries with
it the energy of positivity
to encourage you."

Affirmation	Comfort & Reassurance	Enjoy the Wonder	Financial Reassurance	Hello from Heaven	Time for Life Review

My Story

_____

_____

_____

_____

_____

_____

_____

_____

Date found: _____ Coin #_____

Where: _____

What or who I was thinking about :

_____

_____

Year of coin:

Tails up

        Heads up

The Coin

"Finding a lot of coins
in a very short time frame
is an invitation for you to
consider whether your life
has become out of
balance."

Date found: _____ Coin #_____

Where: _____

What or who I was thinking about :

_____

_____

Year of coin:

Tails up

Heads up

My Story

_____

_____

_____

_____

_____

_____

_____

Affirmation	Comfort & Reassurance	Enjoy the Wonder	Financial Reassurance	Hello from Heaven	Time for Life Review

19

"What if every
time you found a coin
in a most unusual way
you understood that
you'd just been invited
to enjoy a state of
wonder?"

Affirmation	Comfort & Reassurance	Enjoy the Wonder	Financial Reassurance	Hello from Heaven	Time for Life Review

My Story

_____

_____

_____

_____

_____

_____

_____

Date found: _____ Coin #_____

Where: _____

What or who I was thinking about :

_____

_____

Year of coin:

Tails up

Heads up

The Coin

"Stop in the moment
you find a coin and allow
yourself to soak in the magic
of the experience. Lean
into the reassurance that
you are not alone."

Date found: _____ Coin #_____

Where: _____

What or who I was thinking about :

_____

_____

Year of coin:

The Coin

Tails up

Heads up

My Story

_____

_____

_____

_____

_____

_____

_____

Affirmation	Comfort & Reassurance	Enjoy the Wonder	Financial Reassurance	Hello from Heaven	Time for Life Review

"Coins provide a way
for our loved ones in
Heaven to continue
interacting, an inlet
through which to offer
their love and support."

Affirmation	Comfort & Reassurance	Enjoy the Wonder	Financial Reassurance	Hello from Heaven	Time for Life Review

My Story

_____

_____

_____

_____

_____

_____

_____

Date found: _____ Coin #_____

Where: _____

What or who I was thinking about :

_____

_____

Year of coin:

Tails up

Heads up

The Coin

"A coin found when you are feeling disillusioned with life invites you to rediscover the value of wonder, the inspiration it offers and its healing benefits."

Date found: _____ Coin # _____

Where: _____

What or who I was thinking about :

_____

_____

Year of coin:

The Coin

Tails up

Heads up

My Story

_____
_____
_____
_____
_____
_____
_____
_____

Affirmation	Comfort & Reassurance	Enjoy the Wonder	Financial Reassurance	Hello from Heaven	Time for Life Review

"The mystery
and fun of things that
are unexplainable...
this is the magic
of life."

Affirmation	Comfort & Reassurance	Enjoy the Wonder	Financial Reassurance	Hello from Heaven	Time for Life Review

My Story

_____

_____

_____

_____

_____

_____

_____

Date found: _____ Coin # _____

Where: _____

What or who I was thinking about :

_____

_____

Year of coin:

Tails up

Heads up

The Coin

29

"A coin appearing where no coin could possibly be is a little miracle in itself. It serves to increase your awareness of miracles, thereby inviting more miracles into your life."

Date found: _____ Coin #_____

Where: _____

What or who I was thinking about :

_____

_____

Year of coin:

The Coin

Tails up

Heads up

My Story

_____

_____

_____

_____

_____

_____

_____

Affirmation	Comfort & Reassurance	Enjoy the Wonder	Financial Reassurance	Hello from Heaven	Time for Life Review

"In order to receive divine help it's beneficial to be in a state of faith. Coins stamped In God We Trust are the perfect reminder to put our faith back into the Creator."

Affirmation	Comfort & Reassurance	Enjoy the Wonder	Financial Reassurance	Hello from Heaven	Time for Life Review

My Story

_____

_____

_____

_____

_____

_____

_____

Date found: _____ Coin #_____

Where: _____

What or who I was thinking about :

_____

_____

Year of coin:

Tails up

Heads up

The Coin

"It is totally possible to reconnect to the vibrancy of life by noticing the unusual placement of a coin and allowing that sense of wonder in."

Date found: _____ Coin #_____

Where: _____

What or who I was thinking about :

_____

_____

Year of coin:

The Coin

Tails up

Heads up

My Story

_____

_____

_____

_____

_____

_____

_____

Affirmation	Comfort & Reassurance	Enjoy the Wonder	Financial Reassurance	Hello from Heaven	Time for Life Review

"If you begin to find coins every single day, everywhere you go, heavenly support is in place to help you make healthy life changes."

Affirmation	Comfort & Reassurance	Enjoy the Wonder	Financial Reassurance	Hello from Heaven	Time for Life Review

My Story

_____

_____

_____

_____

_____

_____

_____

_____

Date found: _____ Coin #_____

Where: _____

What or who I was thinking about :

_____

_____

Year of coin:

Tails up

Heads up

The Coin

37

"The coin that serves as an affirmation may give you the sensation of your heart expanding with warmth and joy."

Date found: _____ Coin #_____

Where: _____

What or who I was thinking about :

_____

_____

Year of coin:

Tails up

Heads up

My Story

_____

_____

_____

_____

_____

_____

_____

Affirmation	Comfort & Reassurance	Enjoy the Wonder	Financial Reassurance	Hello from Heaven	Time for Life Review

"Coins found during times of illness serve to shift our thoughts away from illness into wonder. Wonder reminds us that anything is possible, including miracles."

Affirmation	Comfort & Reassurance	Enjoy the Wonder	Financial Reassurance	Hello from Heaven	Time for Life Review

My Story

_____

_____

_____

_____

_____

_____

_____

_____

Date found: _____ Coin # _____

Where: _____

What or who I was thinking about :

_____

_____

Year of coin:

Tails up

Heads up

The Coin

"Your guides and angels are willing to help you bring more joy and awe into your life and await your invitation to do so."

Date found: _____ Coin #_____

Where: _____

What or who I was thinking about :

_____

_____

Year of coin:

The Coin

Tails up

Heads up

My Story

_____

_____

_____

_____

_____

_____

_____

Affirmation	Comfort & Reassurance	Enjoy the Wonder	Financial Reassurance	Hello from Heaven	Time for Life Review

"Every coin
you find is more than
just an invitation to a
divine conversation.
It's also a gift of
wonder."

Affirmation	Comfort & Reassurance	Enjoy the Wonder	Financial Reassurance	Hello from Heaven	Time for Life Review

My Story

_____

_____

_____

_____

_____

_____

_____

Date found: _____ Coin #_____

Where: _____

What or who I was thinking about :

_____

_____

Year of coin:

Tails up

Heads up

The Coin

*"When we stop
to marvel at life's
dazzling moments we
open ourselves to receive
spiritual insight."*

Date found: _____ Coin #_____

Where: _____

What or who I was thinking about :

_____

_____

Year of coin:

The Coin

Tails up

Heads up

My Story

_____

_____

_____

_____

_____

_____

_____

Affirmation	Comfort & Reassurance	Enjoy the Wonder	Financial Reassurance	Hello from Heaven	Time for Life Review

"Finding money
when you're worried
about money is a form of
divine reassurance.
Return to faith and
allow your Creator to
provide."

Affirmation	Comfort & Reassurance	Enjoy the Wonder	Financial Reassurance	Hello from Heaven	Time for Life Review

My Story

_____

_____

_____

_____

_____

_____

_____

Date found: _____ Coin #_____

Where: _____

What or who I was thinking about :

_____

_____

Year of coin:

Tails up

Heads up

The Coin

49

"What expands a one-time, mind-boggling coin finding experience into ongoing communication is your genuine interest in fostering it."

Date found: _____ Coin # _____

Where: _____

What or who I was thinking about :

_____

_____

Year of coin:

Tails up

Heads up

My Story

_____

_____

_____

_____

_____

_____

_____

_____

Affirmation	Comfort & Reassurance	Enjoy the Wonder	Financial Reassurance	Hello from Heaven	Time for Life Review

"If you find coins after a loved one has passed on consider this message: A coin placed on your path carries my love as well as my hope that you'll experience wonder and enjoy life."

Affirmation	Comfort & Reassurance	Enjoy the Wonder	Financial Reassurance	Hello from Heaven	Time for Life Review

My Story

_____

_____

_____

_____

_____

_____

_____

Date found: _____ Coin #_____

Where: _____

What or who I was thinking about :

_____

_____

Year of coin:

Tails up

Heads up

The Coin

53

"If your thoughts
were centered around
an action when you
happened to find a coin,
that coin may be a
positive affirmation
for you."

Date found: _____ Coin #_____

Where: _____

What or who I was thinking about :

_____

_____

Year of coin:

The Coin

Tails up

Heads up

My Story

_____

_____

_____

_____

_____

_____

_____

Affirmation	Comfort & Reassurance	Enjoy the Wonder	Financial Reassurance	Hello from Heaven	Time for Life Review

"If you find coins while you're changing life for the higher good, it's a sign that you're not going it alone."

Affirmation	Comfort & Reassurance	Enjoy the Wonder	Financial Reassurance	Hello from Heaven	Time for Life Review

My Story

_____

_____

_____

_____

_____

_____

_____

Date found: _____ Coin #_____

Where: _____

What or who I was thinking about :

_____

_____

Year of coin:

Tails up

Heads up

The Coin

"If a coin catches your attention when you're in a busy trance, I hope you'll smile to yourself, pick it up and "have a moment."

Date found: _____ Coin #_____

Where: _____

What or who I was thinking about :

_____

_____

Year of coin:

The Coin

Tails up

Heads up

My Story

_____

_____

_____

_____

_____

_____

_____

Affirmation	Comfort & Reassurance	Enjoy the Wonder	Financial Reassurance	Hello from Heaven	Time for Life Review

"A coin found
in the most unlikely of
ways serves to remind you
that anything is possible
in this phenomenal world
of ours."

Affirmation	Comfort & Reassurance	Enjoy the Wonder	Financial Reassurance	Hello from Heaven	Time for Life Review

My Story

_____

_____

_____

_____

_____

_____

_____

_____

Date found: _____ Coin # _____

Where: _____

What or who I was thinking about :

_____

_____

Year of coin:

Tails up

Heads up

The Coin

"To experience wonder with increasing regularity is a sign of spiritual expansion and awakening."

Date found: _____ Coin # _____

Where: _____

What or who I was thinking about :

_____

_____

Year of coin:

The Coin

Tails up

Heads up

My Story

_____
_____
_____
_____
_____
_____
_____

Affirmation	Comfort & Reassurance	Enjoy the Wonder	Financial Reassurance	Hello from Heaven	Time for Life Review

"If you find coins while worried about finances, consider this message: Let go of worry so you may pay attention to the world around you. Solutions often come from unexpected sources."

Affirmation	Comfort & Reassurance	Enjoy the Wonder	Financial Reassurance	Hello from Heaven	Time for Life Review

My Story

_____

_____

_____

_____

_____

_____

_____

Date found: _____ Coin #_____

Where: _____

What or who I was thinking about :

_____

_____

Year of coin:

Tails up

Heads up

The Coin

"The loving hand of
the Divine will reach
out to those running on
auto-pilot, sometimes using
the strange placement
of a coin to bring you back
into the present moment."

Date found: _____ Coin #_____

Where: _____

What or who I was thinking about :

_____

_____

Year of coin:

The Coin

Tails up

Heads up

My Story

_____

_____

_____

_____

_____

_____

_____

Affirmation	Comfort & Reassurance	Enjoy the Wonder	Financial Reassurance	Hello from Heaven	Time for Life Review

"Coins that serve as affirmations often show up quite randomly. Like a hint from the ethers, they seem to whisper: Psst. You're headed the right way."

Affirmation	Comfort & Reassurance	Enjoy the Wonder	Financial Reassurance	Hello from Heaven	Time for Life Review

My Story

_____

_____

_____

_____

_____

_____

_____

Date found: _____ Coin # _____

Where: _____

What or who I was thinking about :

_____

_____

Year of coin:

Tails up

Heads up

The Coin

"Throw your arms open wide to wonder offered to you by a found coin. Within its energetic embrace, wonder wraps you in the energy of hope, awe, healing and inspiration."

Date found: _____ Coin #_____

Where: _____

What or who I was thinking about :

_____

_____

Year of coin:

The Coin

Tails up

Heads up

My Story

_____

_____

_____

_____

_____

_____

_____

Affirmation	Comfort & Reassurance	Enjoy the Wonder	Financial Reassurance	Hello from Heaven	Time for Life Review

"By placing your
attention on what is
wondrous about life,
you nurture an intuitive
conversation that, if
honored, will enrich your
life deeply."

Affirmation	Comfort & Reassurance	Enjoy the Wonder	Financial Reassurance	Hello from Heaven	Time for Life Review

My Story

_____

_____

_____

_____

_____

_____

_____

Date found: _____ Coin # _____

Where: _____

What or who I was thinking about :

_____

_____

Year of coin:

Tails up

Heads up

The Coin

Continued from page number:

Continued from page number:

Continued from page number:

Continued from page number:

Continued from page number:

Continued from page number:

Continued from page number:

Continued from page number:

Continued from page number:

Continued from page number:

Continued from page number:

Continued from page number:

Continued from page number:

ABOUT THE AUTHOR

In 2010, Kimberly Ahri began to find coins everywhere, every single day. This curious experience lasted for weeks, prompting her to pray for guidance and ask the question, "Is there meaning in finding coins?"

The answer changed her life and initiated a wonder-filled journey that infused her weary spirit during some of her most challenging times with chronic illness.

Kimberly found herself on a journey with angels. This odyssey, replete with experience, loss, and love, took her through an emotional masterclass on what truly matters in life. The spiritual curriculum required that she look deep within and allow the emergence of her intuitive gifts so she could honor her purpose in this world.

Although she's a very private person by nature, she began writing about her amazing experiences with the coins as an answer to her calling. It was clear. Messages of love, wonder, and connection are meant to be shared.

Kimberly is a health researcher and hope addict; a lover of clean food, clean breathing, sunshine, the ocean, the scenery and good people of Newfoundland, almond milk lattes, sourdough bread, and real butter.

She can be reached at KimberlyAhri.com, where she continues to offer creations based in based in love, compassion, and honor.

Experience the Wonder!

Here's what Amazon readers have been saying about

The Meaning of Finding Coins: Messages and Spiritual Insights

"This book absolutely spoke to me. I felt reaffirmed by so many passages and then learned so much from others. It's filled with stories of people just like me that find coins from loved ones who have passed. I also love how the writer guides you to personal enrichment in an easy to understand way, with tips and steps we can take toward personal enlightenment. This book leaves you feeling hopeful, loved and inspired. So insightful and well written."

"This book has been its own rare and priceless 'coin-find.'"

"This book really encouraged me to stop and take in the wonder of a Universe so much larger than what I can see in front of my face. I no longer ignore pennies on the ground..."

"Kimberly's (book) was just what I needed and now I am confident of the messages being delivered to me in the form of pennies! I hope that she makes as much of a difference in your life as she has in mine!"

"Its message is so much bigger than its title... it has inspired me to become more mindful of messages that may be trying to reach me; alighting my heart with a renewed appreciation of the power of magical wonder."

"The author does a wonderful job of combining personal inspiration along with the testimonies of others. This book is very uplifting and encouraging."

In this enchanting book, Kimberly shares the personal story and deeply comforting angelic messages that began her own coin-finding journey. Step into a world of wonder. Warm your heart with true miracle stories and get the expanded information that will help you discern what your personal messages are in the coins you find.